Bountiful Hearts

Part of the

ABUNDANT *Faith* WOMEN'S BIBLE STUDY SERIES

Herald Press
Harrisonburg, Virginia
Kitchener, Ontario

Library of Congress Cataloging-in-Publication Data
Bountiful hearts.
pages cm. -- (Abundant faith: women's Bible study series)
ISBN 978-1-5138-0025-7 (pbk. : alk. paper) 1. Wealth--Biblical teaching. 2. Money--Biblical teaching. 3. Christian women--Religious life.
BS680.W38B68 2016
241'.68--dc23
2015028896

Library of Congress Control Number: 2015028896
International Standard Book Number: 978-1-5138-0025-7
Printed in the United States of America
Cover and interior design: Merrill Miller
Writer: Patricia Burdette
Printed in the USA

Content for the Abundant Faith Bible study series has been sponsored jointly by Mennonite Women USA, Mennonite Women Canada, and MennoMedia. Mennonite Women USA and Mennonite Women Canada encourage women to nurture their life in Christ, share their gifts, support each other, and engage in mission and service.

Mennonite Women

Mennonite Women Canada

To order or request information, please call 1-800-245-7894 or visit www.MennoMedia.org.

20 19 18 17 16 15 10 9 8 7 6 5 4 3 2 1

Herald Press

CONTENTS

Preface

THOUGH I was honored to be asked to write this guide, I was also intimidated by the subject matter: money. As a pastor's wife, I have heard many a pastor observe that people in the church are far more reluctant to discuss money than they are to talk about sex. Money is an extremely intimate subject for most of us. My initial concern was that some might be put off by the subject and not even read the guide. I sincerely hope this is not the case, for the Bible has much to say on the subject. If we fail to listen we may fail to understand the whole gospel message.

When I first sat down to write this guide, I began by looking at what Scripture has to say about money. At first, I thought I might not find enough material for thirteen sessions, but I could not have been more mistaken! Jesus alone has many more teachings on the subject than I could cover here. Writing this study has significantly affected my own attitudes toward money, toward the way God blesses us with money, and toward the responsibilities that come with the blessing of money. Charity and generosity have taken on a new meaning for me as I read what God says about money. I hope that you, too, will find yourself listening to Jesus' words about money and perhaps begin to look at your own blessing of money in a new way.

—Patricia Burdette

A Word on the Use of This Guide

SPIRITUAL GROWTH involves learning to know God through the Scriptures and through life experience. The sessions allow women to deepen their faith through biblical study and personal reflection.

Overview: introduces the session;

Visual: provides visual and worship focus;

Gathering: focuses attention with stories, questions, or in other ways;

Deepening: reflects on Scripture;

Integrating: asks questions for pondering and discussion; and

Closing: gives scriptural insights and life lessons in an atmosphere of prayer.

Women can use this guide in a variety of ways

1. **Both individual reflection and group sharing.** Women read the sessions during the week, or at the beginning of the meeting time, and choose one or two questions to ponder. In the group setting, each participant might then share her thoughts and insights with the others. This approach recognizes that group sharing is deeply enriched through time for personal reflection. The role of the leader is to facilitate sharing rather than to "teach" the sessions. The leader will need to focus on one or two questions rather than trying to include them all.

   Group participants could be encouraged to journal or use another art form to express their response to the material in each session. If the participants enjoy preparing in advance, sharing their previous days or weeks reflections would be helpful in challenging one another to new insights about the material.

2. **An individual or informal study.** An individual can study the Bible text and meditate on the words, perhaps using a journal to make entries and notice how God is walking with her. Or a group of friends may sit around the kitchen table and study the sessions together.

3. **A more traditional approach.** For a more formal Bible study, the makeup of the group is essential to the format the leader chooses. A teaching group is more likely to emphasize the Deepening section rather than the Integrating questions, which are quite personal in nature. Here are a few questions a leader might use to promote interaction with the material presented in the Deepening section:

- How have you understood this passage in the past?
- What is new or different about the ideas presented here?
- What do you find interesting or intriguing?
- What makes you uncomfortable?
- What feelings do you notice as you reflect on this lesson?
- How might the Spirit be inviting you to grow?

4. **Shorter meditations.** The group or individual might want to use only the Overview, Visual, and Gathering for shorter meditations. Some women might prefer sharing stories and memories sparked by the Gathering section. Others will enjoy responding to the question, "If you were the teacher, what would you emphasize in this lesson, or from this Scripture passage?" Still others might like to read the Scripture, spend a few moments in silent reflection, and close with a song or prayer.

Whatever the makeup of the group, pray for spiritual growth in an atmosphere of trust, confidentiality, and respect. As women of faith, may we grow in confidence and wisdom as we receive our gifts from God and share them with others.

ONE

Rethinking Money

READING: Mark 2:21-22

OVERVIEW

In this parable, Jesus uses a common example with which all in his audience are familiar—cloth and mending. Today, most women no longer mend cloth; even fewer make wine and put it into wineskins. In Jesus' day this parable suggested something radically new.

Both cloth and wine were valuable to Jesus' audience, and women took care as they mended cloth. As women made wine, they knew they could not use old skins to hold it; as the wine fermented it would expand, causing the previously stretched wineskins to burst. The 1970s expression "That blows my mind" captures the idea that the mind figuratively explodes as it tries to comprehend a completely new idea.

In this parable Jesus uses items and concepts familiar to his audience to teach them that being in relationship with

God is something that requires a completely new way of thinking. We need to start over, be born again, and think in a new way. Otherwise, we will not be able to grasp the radical way of living Jesus proposes.

New ways of thinking seem to be no easier today than they were in Jesus' time two thousand years ago. For each of us, the way we think about money begins at a very early age; our thought patterns do not readily change. Jesus teaches that we should not concern ourselves with having enough money for food, clothing, and shelter, but about being in right relationship with God and others. This is truly "mind-blowing." The parable of the new wineskins calls us to completely rethink our attitudes about money and, in fact, about life. Could this be what conversion really means?

VISUAL: a piece of old cloth with a patch on it

GATHERING

A poster had an impact on me. With it's colorful red and blue background, it brought a new translation of a familiar Scripture, Romans 12:2: "Do not be conformed to this world, but be transformed by the renewing of your minds." The poster read "Don't let the world squeeze you into its mold, but be transformed with a new way of thinking." As I read this, I understood that being a Christian is not just about what we do or don't do; it is about seeing the world more as God sees it—in a whole new way.

This insight had a profound impact on my family when we volunteered with a church agency for a number of years. Not only did it help us view the poor and needy in a new way, we were also confronted with social structures that privilege some while oppressing others. We came to realize that money in North American society is equivalent to power. Those who are most concerned about food, clothing, and shelter often have little power in our society. But that is something they share with Jesus, who did not concern himself with money and, as a result, did not have worldly power. We learned that we needed to rethink our personal relationship with money in order to be in right relationship with God.

DEEPENING

Living in a culture that seems to revolve around consumerism presents unique obstacles for Christians to overcome. Sometimes this is complicated with a commitment to simple living, or living simply. Does living simply mean having what everyone else in our society has, but getting it at bargain prices? Or does it mean forgoing some consumer items because they are not necessary no matter how good the bargain? Does it mean that it is okay to have frivolous consumer items if we purchase them at a fair trade store, a thrift store, or at a fundraising event? Does it mean we must put hundreds of thousands of dollars in savings for our church in order to be good stewards, or does it mean spending most of that money for ministry in our own communities?

There are no easy answers to these questions, yet these are the kinds of questions we need to ask our families, our congregations, and ourselves. As the Holy Spirit helps us to use the principles Jesus teaches, and as we rethink our relationship with money, this spiritual growth can be a "mind-blowing" experience. It will also draw us closer to God, and it can be a way to usher in the kingdom of God.

INTEGRATING

1. Silently consider a time the Holy Spirit transformed your thinking about food, clothing, or shelter. Was the transformation a slow process, or was it a powerful change, done in an instant? Try to remember as many details of the experience as you can. Reflect silently; then anyone who wishes may share her thoughts.

2. When do you first remember discussing money with another person? How do some of your early memories of money continue to be a part of your attitude about money today?

3. Do you think Christians would be more thoughtful about money if they had a financial accountability group to discuss areas such as family budget, future events to save for, or charitable causes to support? Would you spend money differently if you had such a group? How can the church help us have a biblically focused attitude toward money?

CLOSING

The Holy Spirit prompts us to grow in our faith and our relationship with God and transforms us. Ask someone who knows you well to tell you ways they have seen your faith growing. If you are part of a group, take turns sharing in smaller groups how you have seen the Spirit transforming one of the women, or how you see the Spirit transforming you.

TWO

Finding the Kingdom

READING: Matthew 13:44-45

OVERVIEW

Jesus tells a series of parables, each beginning with the words "the kingdom of God is like . . ." It's like someone who finds a treasure in a field, then sells all she owns to purchase that field; or like a merchant who finds a pearl of great value and sells all she owns to purchase it. In each case, the person who finds the item of value sells all that she owns to possess the most valuable of all possessions, which is the kingdom of God.

Are we to sell all that we own for the kingdom of God? Probably not. So what is Jesus teaching us? Here, as in many other teachings, Jesus is simply using a figure of speech to help make his subject more accessible. The purpose of all figurative language is to suggest a resemblance or link between two otherwise distinct objects and thus convey a larger, more complex idea. For example, a figure of speech we might use is "a tie in a soccer match is like kissing your dog." Soccer and dogs are not usually linked together.

Some figures of speech are so overused that they become clichés, but we still understand their meaning. For example, we say things like "She is thin as a rail" or "Better late than never." These figures of speech have been used and reused, but at some point, they were brand new.

In this chapter, Jesus created new figures of speech to teach the concept of the kingdom of God. In verse 13, Jesus explains to the disciples that he speaks to the crowds in parables because "seeing they do not perceive, and hearing they do not listen, nor do they understand." Jesus was indeed a master storyteller.

VISUAL: a large pearl on a small piece of dark velvet fabric

GATHERING

There is a story of a woman who finds a valuable pearl in an obscure shop. The merchant says he will give it to the woman in exchange for everything she has. Wanting badly to own the pearl, she writes out a check for several thousand dollars, emptying her savings and checking accounts. Then the merchant asks, "What about your house?" The woman signs over the deed. "What about your two cars?" She signs them both over to him. "What about your boat and your vacation home? Your stocks and bonds, retirement funds, life insurance?" The woman transfers all of these to the merchant.

Then the merchant says, "Now the pearl is yours." The woman is delighted! She turns to leave with her treasure, but the merchant stops her saying, "Here is all that you have given me to purchase the pearl; I am giving it to you. It still belongs to me, but I will let you have full use of it for as long as you live. The only thing I ask is that sometimes you share my houses, cars, and other wealth with those I send your way." The woman is overcome with joy, "Of course, thank you!"

"Remember," says the merchant, "you may use these things as if they are your own, but on occasion, I will ask you to share them with others."

DEEPENING

The story of the pearl is a metaphor—a figure of speech in which a word or phrase that is not literally applicable is used to represent something in the real world. What do you think the pearl represents? What about the shop? The woman? The merchant? How is this story like Jesus' parable? What is different about our lives and possessions today, compared to Jesus' day?

When I first heard this story, I immediately saw myself as the woman purchasing the pearl. It made me realize how much I own and how much God has given me. I saw that my possessions were not for me alone, but were meant to be shared with others in need. Before, I might have felt I deserved all of this wealth because I was a good, hardworking Christian rewarded by God. Now, I saw my wealth—my money, my home, my car, or other possessions—in a new way. I am like a trustee who holds something valuable for the true owner.

It was as if a weight had been lifted from my shoulders.

This new understanding seemed to create a whole new relationship between me and my possessions. It was as if a weight had been lifted from my shoulders. When volunteering full time with a church agency, we had the use of money, a home, and a car, but they were not really ours. They actually belonged to the agency and were to be used for serving in the name of Christ. All at once, I realized how similar my current situation was to my experience when volunteering. My wealth was not really my own, but God's, and it was to be used to serve in the name of Christ in my own community.

INTEGRATING

1. At the beginning of the story of the woman purchasing the pearl, did you find yourself thinking that this woman was seriously flawed? How did you react when she began signing over titles for her homes, cars, boat, and other items to the merchant? Did the woman seem foolish to you at the beginning of the story? What about at the end? What changes did your attitude toward her undergo as the story progressed?

2. Why do you think Jesus' parable and the story both use the idea of exchanging all of a person's possessions for the kingdom of God? What material things have you let go of in order to participate more fully in God's calling in your life?

3. Share your understanding of Jesus' parable.

CLOSING

Give each person a pencil and a piece of paper about the size of a note card. Have each woman create a present-day figure of speech to describe the kingdom of God: "The kingdom of God is like . . ." After about five minutes, have each woman fold her paper and place it in a small basket. Take turns drawing a paper from the basket and reading the simile to the rest of the group.

THREE

God's Economics

READING: Mark 12:41-44

OVERVIEW

In today's gospel story, Jesus observes people making financial contributions as they enter the synagogue. He calls his disciples to him and points out that a poor widow has contributed all she has to the offering. He uses this woman as an example of one who makes a true sacrifice to God.

We see that Jesus has a way of turning everything in his world on its head to explain God's perspective. We see that God's economics are drastically different from those of the larger culture. In this Scripture, we are told that God looks at what we give in comparison to what we actually have. Yet in Jesus' time, as in our own, most look at the size of the contribution alone. Jesus seems to be asking us to rethink our definition of generosity.

It is often difficult to consider how different the life of a widow in Jesus' time was from most widows' lives today. There was no financial safety net of government and community programs, no church agencies to help. There was no pension system for widows, built up as a result of their own years of work or their deceased husband's retirement plan. Widows were absolutely at the mercy of the generosity of their sons, if they had sons, or other community members.

VISUAL: a simple plate or dish containing one penny

GATHERING

Imagine how much this widow needed the contribution she gave to the synagogue for her own survival. Now consider your life. If you are single, consider what provisions you have made for the future. If you are married, consider what financial arrangements have been made to care for your needs if your spouse should die before you. If you are a widow, consider what arrangements were made to care for your needs. How do you see your circumstances as being similar or different from the widow in this story? How do your fears affect your generosity?

DEEPENING

In Jesus' time, women were considered significantly inferior to men. It was important for a woman to have a man (father, uncle, husband, son) to protect her and care for her. During this time, poverty was considered a punishment for sin. Imagine the reaction most people would have had to a poor widow. Given this situation, Jesus' teaching is even more astonishing; he elevated her!

Today, of course, we do not see poverty as punishment for sin. Or do we?

Today, of course, we do not see poverty as punishment for sin. Or do we? Is poverty the consequence of sinful living? Jesus does not teach this. In fact, Jesus points out this powerless widow as an example of what it means to give abundantly to God, not as an example of judgment on sin.

Whenever I read this Scripture, I visualize Ruby as the poor widow. Lifelong churchgoers, Ruby and her husband had six children before he became permanently disabled. Ruby was a widow when I met her, and even with her children raised to middle age, she lived on a meager income. But each week, Ruby contributed to the offering.

I will never forget Ruby's comment about tithing during a church study on stewardship. She said, "The tithe is just the first 10 percent of everything, but it is not the offering. The tithe *already* belongs to God, but the offering is what you give of the 90 percent that is yours to spend however you choose. The offering is where you can make a sacrifice to God."

This comment struck me like a thunderbolt. Would I have given a tithe, let alone an offering, in her circumstances? Ruby believed that her faithfulness in giving both the tithe and the offering was a way for God to remind her repeatedly of *God's* faithfulness as she raised her family.

I have heard that most people would rather discuss their sexual life with others than their finances. But discussing the use of the gifts God has so generously given seems an appropriate area of discernment for the community of believers.

The stories of the widow and Ruby show how, when people are poor, their incomes seem to be more transparent. Wealthy persons may hide their check ledgers, and keep their spending habits hidden. Yet, even if we are wealthy, our homes, furnishings, pets, cars, clothing, appearances, vacations, and hospitality practices reflect our wealth and are often used to impress others. This was true in Jesus' time, also. Could Jesus have been urging people to be more open and transparent about their use of money?

INTEGRATING

1. Jesus does not tell us what we must give—only that we are to treat others as we treat ourselves. How do our fears and concerns for our financial future affect our generosity?

2. Some Christians today hold the same views as the Jews of Jesus' day: wealth is a blessing and poverty a punishment. Discuss the merits or shortcomings of this view.

3. Jesus tells his disciples that the poor widow has contributed more than all the others contributing to the synagogue because they are giving from their abundance while she is giving from her poverty. If all Christians gave more like the widow, what do you think the church would be like? How would this generosity affect transparency about money?

4. Share stories from your own experiences that are similar to Ruby's.

CLOSING

Have each woman take a penny or other coin from her purse and place it in her right hand. Lead them in a guided exercise of imagination: Imagine that this is the only money you have. Close your eyes and see yourself as the poor widow, dependent on others. You place your last coin in the offering container. You have faith that God will provide for your future financial needs, if not for your wants. Open your eyes. Look up to God and declare, "I have the faith to tithe and give an offering, too."

FOUR

Gifts for God

READING: Luke 8:1-3

OVERVIEW

Have you wondered how Jesus managed the logistics of his ministry? In today's Scripture, we find women traveling with Jesus who have received his healing touch. They believe Jesus is the Messiah, and they know how much Jesus has changed their lives for the better. We are told that these women provide for Jesus and the disciples using their own resources. This could mean sharing intelligence, personal connections, strength, and skill, but it primarily refers to money. No one can survive without it, no matter how frugal or self-sufficient.

Historically, women have not had a great deal of control over money, yet these women do. They are single as well as married, and they choose to use their own means to provide for Jesus and the disciples. This generous act makes it possible for Jesus to take his ministry to cities and villages in the area. Through their generosity, these women contributed significantly to the beginnings of the Christian church.

VISUAL: ten fifty-cent pieces or other silver coins in an offering plate

GATHERING

When I was a child our family did not attend church, but I spent six years as a foster child, and my foster family attended church often. Although I was young, I remember the small white church building sitting close to the side of a dirt road surrounded by nothing but deep green fields and trees. The church had two stained-glass windows, which made colorful designs on the walls, pews, and floor of the sanctuary. My Sunday school class took place in the choir loft, and I have vivid memories of children taking out their offering money and of the sparkles of color the light created as it struck the coins.

I always sat beside the pastor's daughter and watched her reach into her change purse for coins. In those days, fifty-cent pieces were common; the pastor's daughter had so many of them in her change purse, my eyes nearly popped out of my head when I saw them. I thought she must be the richest person I knew. She always put one or two of these large coins in the offering plate.

I am still amazed when I think of a six-year-old carrying that much money, even if it's not worth much today. Yet someone had taught this young child the importance of being generous, to help the good news of God's kingdom continue to spread throughout our nation and world. I like to think that as an adult, this young girl I remember so well still has access to money, and that she has continued to be generous to the church, just as the women in today's Scripture were generous. Even if she does not have financial wealth, I am certain she uses whatever gifts God provides to serve her Lord.

DEEPENING

Jesus' band must have included quite a group of people traveling on foot, along with some donkeys to carry supplies. It must have been like a primitive campout each time they stopped for a meal or a night's rest. In that culture, the women would have had to collect firewood, make a fire, and find food to prepare. The women would then prepare and serve the food, and clean up after the meal. They would have had to wash and mend the men's clothing and make certain everyone had bedding for the night. Nonetheless, the women voluntarily traveled with the men, provided for them, and used their own money to do so.

This is asking quite a lot from women. How many of us would willingly make such a sacrifice? Thankfully, we don't have to. Today, traveling evangelists have staff to telephone ahead to arrange hotel accommodations, set up banquets, send out press releases, and drop off laundry. But I suspect many of these helpers are women.

Jesus consistently reaches out to women in ways that empower them to use their gifts in the newly forming church.

When I think about the social structures in Jesus' day, I think of women as being near the bottom. Yet Jesus consistently reaches out to women in ways that empower them to use their gifts in the newly forming church. Joanna, the text tells us, is the wife of Herod's steward; she probably used her social connections to assist the group as they traveled. Mary Magdalene and Susanna are also named in this passage, along with "many others" whose gifts are used to benefit Jesus' community and mission.

We may not think of the money we control as a gift. We typically think of money as a necessity that pays the rent and utilities, buys the groceries and clothing we require, and helps us transport ourselves. But the ability to use money to provide for Jesus' work today is really a gift. Many women in our world, even in North America, have little wealth. Women in the United States and Canada still do not earn as much as their male counterparts, and women are still not readily welcome in certain professions. Jesus, however, did not treat women as inferior; he encouraged them to use their gifts, and in so doing, he gave women life. Women gifted with money gave generously in return, so that Jesus' life-giving love could change others' lives, as it had changed their own.

INTEGRATING

1. What are some of your earliest memories of Sunday school? Do you recall if you had an offering? If so, how much money was given and how generous were you and your classmates?

2. What gifts do you feel called to use to extend God's kingdom? Have these gifts been affirmed by others? If so, how does that affirmation affect you?

3. If you could serve the church in any capacity, what gift would you choose to have and to use? Explain why.

CLOSING

Take a few minutes to think about the gifts you see in others. Send a note to a woman whose gifts you want to affirm.

FIVE

Guarding against Affluenza

READING: Luke 12:15-21

OVERVIEW

In this reading, Jesus warns against greed and tells the story of a rich man who becomes even wealthier as his land becomes more productive. The man has such an abundant harvest that he runs out of space to store it. To remedy this problem, the rich man plans to build larger barns to store all of his grain and goods. As the rich man plans ways to save his wealth so that he can rest, relax, and have fun for many years, he is unaware that his life will soon end. God calls this rich man a fool. Jesus tells his audience that those who store up treasures for themselves but fail to be rich toward God are also fools.

VISUAL: a large color photograph symbolizing poverty

GATHERING

When I was young, I loved to visit with my grandmother, who lived with us. Her room contained a bed, a dresser, and a cedar chest. In the chest, Grandma kept a few special possessions that I always wanted to look at. I loved to see her carefully remove each item, remind me of its significance as she allowed me to touch it, and tell me its story. Often, this story would lead to another memory of her childhood; those were also stories I loved to hear again and again.

"Those who need lots of things are spiritually weak; those who are close to God don't need very much in this world. Think about it."

When Grandma died at ninety-four, she still had those same few possessions. By this time, I was an adult with children of my own, and somehow it seemed that she should have more possessions to show after such a long life. But then I remembered what Grandma used to tell me: "Those who need lots of things are spiritually weak; those who are close to God don't need very much in this world. Think about it."

What does it mean to be rich toward God? Does it mean giving more generously to the church? Spending time praying, rather than redecorating or shopping? *Rich* has a variety of nuanced meanings, one of which is "pure," as in a rich vein of ore. Another is "meaningful," as in a rich understanding. Perhaps Jesus is telling us that the most important purpose in life is not to seek more things but to enrich our relationship with God, devoting time to God and to God's priorities.

DEEPENING

In this reading, Jesus lets his audience know that keeping up with the Joneses can be a dangerous and foolish preoccupation. He warns us to "be on your guard against all kinds of greed," indicating that this is a danger we may not immediately recognize. Perhaps he is warning his audience of the seductiveness of materialism.

It is difficult in our consumer society to know when we have accumulated enough of anything. Do we need to have all the dishes required to feed the extended family only once a year? Or do we need a special set for Christmas? How many investments do we need as a hedge against poverty? Do we need more than one home? Do we need to add onto our existing home to make room for all of our stuff? How many bathrooms do we need? How many vacations are appropriate? We all know many people whose excesses are much greater than our own! Yet as we watch television and read magazines, these excesses can start to seem normal.

Normalization follows on the heels of marketing strategies that create *perceived need.* First, for example, we are convinced that we could use three bathrooms in our house, and then we are convinced that everyone else has three bathrooms in their house. We are easily convinced that our home will be more marketable with three bathrooms. Therefore, we need to have more bathrooms. In this way, we find ourselves seduced into having much more than we actually need.

We tell ourselves that we are manipulated by advertising agencies, but the real problem, according to Jesus, is that in storing up these treasures for ourselves, we are not being rich towards God. What a stinging indictment of our consumer society!

We can make excuses for the way we give in to consumerism, but this drive for more and more seems to be one of those difficult teachings that Jesus is clear about, not ambiguous. We don't need to feel guilty, but we do need to be on our guard when it comes to our wealth. As Jesus often reminds us, our goal as believers is to love others—not just our immediate family members—as much as we love ourselves.

INTEGRATING

1. Silently recall the last time you worried about not having enough money saved for the future. How did your reasoning about your savings sound similar to that of the rich man in this parable? Following silence, you may wish to share your experiences with the group.

2. What does being rich toward God mean for us, our families, our churches, and our communities? If we truly followed the advice of Jesus in this passage, how might our accumulated wealth change?

3. It is easy to accept that our wealth is the result of our own shrewd actions and decisions, but in the parable, wealth grows because the land becomes more productive. How much of our wealth in North America derives from God's provision rather than our own efforts? How might God wish us to express our thanks?

CLOSING

Prayer:

God whose justice shines like the sun, you bless all who seek first your kingdom and righteousness. Fill our hearts with the spirit of the Beatitudes, that we may live this day in simplicity, mercy, and joy.

SIX

My Spirit Rejoices

READING: Luke 1: 45-55

OVERVIEW

Mary's song is one of four found in the book of Luke, all of which resemble the psalms. This song, in fact, contains references to seven different psalms. In it, Mary praises God for the great blessing of being chosen to bear the Messiah. Verses 51-53 most clearly apply to issues of wealth and poverty. Mary repeats what the Psalms and the prophetic books have said: God favors charity and humility, but punishes greed and arrogance.

VISUAL: a portion of an unsliced loaf of bread on a simple plate or cutting board

GATHERING

I teach a course that covers five hundred years of cultural, intellectual, and political history of Western civilization. One after another, we read of historical figures whose art, ideas, and quests for power have risen and fallen. These important historical figures, along with their concepts, are soon dead and gone, replaced by others who pass just as quickly. Yet people continue to believe in the immortality of their dynasties, ideas, wealth, possessions, influence, and power.

When I hear Mary's song and its reminders of God's justice, I think of the words of Black Elk, a Lakota spiritual leader. He asserts that the real world is the spirit world, the world of the unseen. The Lakota, along with some other tribal groups, express their understanding of Black Elk's words with the giveaway. This event accompanies funerals, weddings, womanhood or manhood initiations, and vision quests, along with a host of other occasions, and is a time when wealth is redistributed within the community.

When our daughter was married on the Pine Ridge Reservation, we had a giveaway as part of the wedding re-

If we really believe, like Mary and Black Elk, that the unseen spiritual world is the world that matters most, then the material things of this physical world hold little value for us and can easily be given away.

ception. Everyone who came to the wedding left with a gift of some kind. Some received beautiful quilts or blankets, while others received T-shirts, jackets, Tupperware, towels, dishes, or cases of oil. The giveaway was a way of thanking the community for their help in the wedding and to honor the couple. It also helped the needy while allowing them to keep their dignity. It let the community see faith put into action.

If we really believe, like Mary and Black Elk, that the unseen spiritual world is the world that matters most, then the material things of this physical world hold little value for us and can easily be given away. This is a value that the Lakota and others have incorporated into their culture as a way to keep their focus on God's provision.

DEEPENING

This portion of Scripture is traditionally associated with the weeks before Christmas, but its timeless quality makes it an appropriate meditation for any season. As Mary reminds us that God "has filled the hungry with good things, and sent the rich away empty," I think of the years our family spent living among the poorest of the poor in the United States, the Lakota people of the Pine Ridge Indian Reservation. Many of the Lakota live a life of material poverty, yet they are filled with wisdom, knowledge, compassion, generosity, faith, and kindness.

At Pine Ridge, I saw the precepts of the Scriptures fully lived out in the lives of those around me. I often wondered why I did not see these qualities to a much greater extent among church communities. Perhaps our wealth encourages our lack of generosity, kindness, and faith. Perhaps by "rich," Mary means "complacent."

Eleanor Two Eagle is one special friend from the Pine Ridge days. She is a widow who is the same age my mother would be if she were still alive, but she reminded me of my grandmother. Eleanor had raised nine children of her own, and five grandchildren. These grandsons and our own sons were always at one another's homes, so naturally, Eleanor and I got to know one another well. Eleanor always fed my boys, and I soon found myself asking her for recipes because my sons said she made the best food they had ever tasted.

Eleanor gave me much more than recipes, however; she gave our family blankets, quilts, and food, even though her home was small and crowded and she had difficulty meeting the needs of all the people who lived there. At first, I was embarrassed to accept her generosity, but when I balked at taking her gifts, insisting that she might need them in the future, she reminded me that the Creator had provided for her generously for many, many years. Soon I understood that Eleanor was grateful to us for all the fun times our family and her grandsons shared, and that it was important to her that we accept her gifts graciously. She is one of the most generous women I know. And like Mary, she will be remembered through all generations.

INTEGRATING

1. Remember a time when you praised God for a spiritual blessing that did not pertain to the physical world. Let those who wish to share do so.

2. Who is the most generous woman you know? What makes her generous—the way she shares her time? Her talents? Her money? Her possessions? Share stories of generosity from your life.

3. How does complacency follow wealth? In what ways have you seen greed or lack of charity accompany wealth?

CLOSING

Set a timer for one minute, and during that time write down as many blessings as you can think of, both material and immaterial. Thank God sincerely for all of the blessings God has given you. Pray that you may use them to make the world a more just place for everyone.

SEVEN

Power, Wealth, and Charity

READING: Mark 10:17-27

OVERVIEW

In today's Scripture, we find a young man (whom Luke's gospel calls a young *ruler*) running up to Jesus, asking what he must do to have eternal life. Jesus loves this man, but still tells him the truth—he has to divest himself of his power and give his wealth to the poor in order to enter God's kingdom. Jesus also mentions how difficult it is for those with material wealth to enter the kingdom, but offers the encouragement that with God nothing is impossible. This shocks everyone within earshot, since the rabbis teach that wealth and power in this world are signs of God's blessing.

VISUAL: a tiara (available in toy stores) on a small satin pillow

GATHERING

In the 1950s, there was a daytime television show called *Queen for a Day*. On stage before an audience, the host would interview weeping women telling hard-luck stories. The audience would vote by applause to select the woman who would become "Queen for a Day," which meant she would receive special gifts from the sponsors of the program. The gifts included things like automatic washers and dryers, refrigerators, stoves, dishwashers, and vacation trips for two to Florida or Hawaii.

Today it is difficult to find women in North America who do not own these appliances. It is almost as difficult to find

Are we "young rulers" similar to the man in our Scripture?

women who have not been to Florida or Hawaii. Does this mean we are queens? Are we "young rulers" similar to the man in our Scripture? Would we be willing to sell our amenities and give up our vacations and give the money to the poor? Jesus tells us that wealth and power are not necessarily signs of blessing; they may be a serious impediment to a healthy relationship with God.

When our family served as volunteers with a church agency, we were allowed to take few possessions with us. Besides a backpack for each of us, we brought one suitcase full of books and two suitcases of clothing. Most of what we owned—clothing, furniture, and farm animals—was sold or given away. It felt very freeing to be unburdened of all those possessions! When we arrived at our assignment in Saskatchewan, we lived in public housing.

Living simply as volunteers seemed easier in those years. Today, our community expects that everyone will have cars, homes, computers, and everything they need to keep their equipment properly maintained. It may be easier than ever to be bogged down by our possessions living in our modern world, and too often these possessions become a stumbling block rather than a stepping stone for ourselves or others.

DEEPENING

The young man in today's Scripture tells Jesus that he has kept all of the commandments since he was a child. Jesus loves this man, so attempts to direct him to the source of his spiritual obstacle. The man fails to understand that merely honoring the commandments is not enough; this superficial obedience must be accompanied by spiritual depth, which can only come from knowing the heart of God. This man relies on his wealth and wordly power to protect and sustain him when he should, instead, be relying on God to provide for his needs.

Jesus knows that God loves all people equally and wants those with more to share with those who have little. Jesus is trying to lead the young man closer to God, but like many of us today, the young man is unable to give up his trust in wealth and rely on God alone. He is unable to see that his worldly possessions are not a blessing, but a hindrance to his relationship with God. Jesus knows that a deep relationship with God helps us to be less reliant on worldly wealth and power. Only by being close to God can we enter God's kingdom.

INTEGRATING

1. Ask yourself if there has ever been a time in your life when wealth and power—whether personal, familial, or national—were of no value to you. What circumstances require you to totally rely on God's mercy, love, and compassion? Share your response with one another, as you feel comfortable.

2. How can we develop a close relationship with God? How can such a relationship help us lose our reliance on the world's wealth and power?

CLOSING

Give each person in the group a small slip of paper and a pencil. Have each woman write one obstacle in her life that keeps her from a deeper healing relationship with God. Fold the papers, and place them in a large tin can. Burn the paper, symbolically releasing each woman from the obstacle that keeps her from a deeper walk with God. End with a prayer of thanksgiving.

EIGHT

Social Morality: Do Justice, Love Mercy

READING: Ezekiel 16:48-50

OVERVIEW

These verses are from the first part of Ezekiel, which begins, like most of the prophetic books, by listing God's reasons for breaking his covenant with the Israelites. Here, the word of God explains that the chief sins of Sodom were not sexual sins; they were sins of pride, wealth, complacency, and a failure to care for those in need.

VISUAL: an object that symbolizes poverty, such as an empty piggy bank, a well-worn shirt, or other item

GATHERING

I once knew a woman who had a very unstable marriage, even though her husband was a wealthy professional. She tried to make the marriage work for the sake of her children; in her desperation, she even tried becoming a churchgoing Christian. But as her husband's violence escalated to an extremely dangerous level, she eventually agreed to the dissolution of the marriage. She was alone in the city, and needed the support of her congregation. Instead, she encountered judgmental Christians who wanted nothing to do with her in her time of trouble. She left the church, only to return several years later after she had remarried. Again, she found herself unwelcome because of what some of the congregation perceived as her "sexual impurity." Eventually, she found a church that understood Ezekiel's message: Be humble and care for others in need; accept others without judging them; remember that God is sovereign, and we are not.

DEEPENING

What comes to mind when you hear the word *immorality*? Today, as in the past, it is easy to focus on sexual immorality (or what we have decided to label as sexual immorality), rather than *social* immorality, which includes systemic poverty and economic injustice. In North America, we like to think that poverty is something "over there," beyond our borders. It is easier to think that corrupt third-world governments fail to attend to their impoverished citizens than to recognize the poverty and enormous chasm between rich and poor in our own country. Similarly, the Israelites looked at their neighboring countries and thought, "At least we are not like those people with their sexual immorality." They were blind to their own social and economic immorality.

Through the prophet Ezekiel, God makes it clear that Sodom was destroyed not for sexual immorality, but social immorality. Its citizens were not charitable. They were prideful and did not help those in need; they had an abundance of food and a comparatively easy life, yet were unwilling to

What if Christians focused on fixing their own pride, apathy, and lack of charity, rather than judging the sins of others?

share God's graciousness with others. It is easy to excuse ourselves from being more charitable! Yet, to God, failing to be charitable is at least as serious as sexual immorality. What if Christians focused on fixing their own pride, apathy, and lack of charity, rather than judging the sins of others? Does God call us to social morality above all else?

I have heard it said that death and childbirth never come at a convenient time. I would like to add *service* to the list. How many times have we put off answering a call to feed the hungry or to visit the sick because it is not convenient for us? How many times have we seen others—or ourselves—show every intention of offering a few years of their lives for special service, but never get around to it? Increasing demands of job, family, businesses, mortgages, and other obligations make convenient excuses. It is difficult to set aside what seem like worthy pursuits to follow a special call from God.

Every choice we make in life has an element of sacrifice; by choosing one thing, we choose against something else. Being charitable to others also requires sacrifice on our part. It is often necessary to sacrifice the "good life" to do God's work on earth, and to hold off our personal judgment of others in order to reach those in need of God's healing. Sharing generously with others, as God has generously given to us, may always seem like a sacrifice at the outset, but in the end, it might not only save us from self-judgment. Sharing God's generosity brings us a renewed sense of God's salvation. If Christians were willing to share sacrificially, following the lead of the God who gave up the privileges of heaven on our behalf (Philippians 2:5-11), we could eliminate much of the poverty in our world.

INTEGRATING

1. Before reading the Ezekiel passage, what did you think the "sin of Sodom" was? How did you react when you read this Scripture?

2. Jesus and the prophets remind us repeatedly of our obligation as God's people to share with others, to remain humble, to not oppress others, and to compassionately care for the poor and needy among us. Why do you think God places such a high premium on social morality or social justice?

3. If those who had plenty shared with those who have very little so that all had enough, but none had an overabundance, how would it change the relationships between countries and communities in our world?

CLOSING

Think about agencies in your area that address the needs of local people. Do your congregations support any of them with money, staff, or volunteers? Are there ways that you could become involved and share what you have? Perhaps, as a group, you could think of one way to collectively support one of the agencies, and then do it.

why Lazarus is relieved of suffering while the rich man's suffering is just beginning. Abraham makes it clear to the rich man that the Scriptures should be taken seriously; there are severe consequences for the choices we make in response to the Word of God. Abraham indicates that those who do not follow the spirit of God's laws cannot be convinced to change "even if someone rises from the dead."

VISUAL: purple cloth and fine linen beside a rag

GATHERING

As a child, my clothing was always presentable. I never dressed in rags, and I always had access to dental care and health services such as immunizations, treatment for broken bones, and medicine for childhood diseases. As a young girl, I never really thought of these things as manifestations of wealth until I read this story. It made me think about all of the poor people I noticed in the downtown area where everyone shopped at that time. Some of the poor beggars had no legs, some had no hands, some were blind, and they all begged on the city streets. Today, most are spared this sight as they go to suburban shopping areas. They see only others who look like they do: healthy, well-dressed, well-groomed people who drive newer, well-maintained cars. Communities are arranged so that the wealthy and the poor do not cross paths, even though the gap between them widens each year. The chasm between the poor and the wealthy is greater now than at any time in the past century. Does the fact that we may not see the poor and needy every day relieve us of the responsibility for the welfare of those less fortunate?

DEEPENING

This is a perplexing and unsettling parable. A rich man lives in luxury and never does anything overtly sinful, yet he ends up being tormented in the afterlife, hearing Abraham's scathing admonition, "In your lifetime you received good things, while Lazarus received bad things, but now he is comforted here and you are in agony." What did he do to deserve this torment? The only thing we are told is that poor, sickly Lazarus was at the rich man's gate each day longing to eat the scraps and crumbs that fell from his table. In his luxurious life, the rich man was simply indifferent to the needs of the less fortunate right before him.

Does this mean that we are responsible not only for the sins we commit through our actions, but for the sins we commit through failure to act, as well? Are we to tend to the needs in our own community before all else? Perhaps the message is that we must take God's direction seriously because God is very serious about it: love the Lord with all your strength, all your mind, your heart, and your soul, and *love your neighbor as yourself.*

INTEGRATING

1. For a moment, close your eyes and imagine that you are Lazarus, sick and destitute. You see a wealthy man walk past you without even acknowledging your need. What feelings does this arouse in you? Share your thoughts with others.

2. Have you ever compared your economic reality with the situations of those around you? Do you ever notice if you have more wealth than others? Do you ever notice if you have less wealth than others? How do these thoughts help or hinder your relationship with God?

3. Would it be better for our society if the paths of the rich and the poorest of the poor crossed more frequently? Why or why not? Share your thoughts with others.

4. Brainstorm as a group to find ways we might change our own paths so that we are confronted with the different economic realities among us in our daily lives.

CLOSING

Close your eyes and imagine you are in a city in North America where you are the richest person in the entire city. What is Jesus saying to you?

Prayer:

God, help us to see the world as you see it; give us your eyes to see the needs of the poor and needy among us.

TEN

Give to God

READING: Mark 12:14-17

OVERVIEW

Here we find the Pharisees trying to trick Jesus once again. First, they flatter him in an effort to disarm him. Once his defenses are down, they hope to expose him in some error. Jesus does not fall victim to their empty flattery; instead, he remains steadfast, preaching God's vision for the world. The Pharisees ask if the Jewish law forbids or allows Jewish citizens to pay taxes to the Roman emperor. Jesus knows the Pharisees are attempting to trap him, and asks why they are testing him. Then he gives an ambiguous answer that creates more questions while evading the trap the Pharisees so carefully set for him.

VISUAL: a piece of dark cloth with coins scattered on it

GATHERING

Many years ago, my husband and I knew several people who did not believe that Christians should pay taxes. The non-denominational pastor who led our friends' church had no formal theological training; he said God taught him what he needed to know in a mystical experience on a mountaintop in the western United States.

These people saw the government as evil, and believed it was their Christian duty not to contribute financially to its work. The pastor encouraged them to divest themselves of ownership of homes, cars, and other items most people need to survive in our culture. Possessions were put into special trusts, and ordinary purchases on which most of us pay sales tax were funneled through the church's nontaxable account.

To its credit, the church did create a loving sense of community among its members. They began to rent homes near the church and to send their children to the church-run school. The women worked communally to can meat and vegetables for the coming year, and ran a food, clothing, and furniture ministry for the area in which they were located. The church was truly the center of their lives. Their goal was to create a community like the one described in the book of Acts. The pastor and the members often quoted today's Scripture: "Give to the emperor the things that are the emperor's, and to God the things that are God's." They argued that since everything belongs to God, nothing belongs to the government.

DEEPENING

At first my husband and I were impressed with this church. But it soon became evident that the church's motivational core was fear based. The gospel preached there was one of a soon-to-come nuclear holocaust; the congregation would become the remnant church of the book of Revelation. Everyone had to be in close physical proximity for fast escape to a shelter they had built. Many items from their food, clothing, and furniture ministries went into this large shelter. They feared the government as much as they mistrusted it, creating an ever-present aura of suspicion and stealth among the group.

We realized how easy it is to twist Jesus' words in ways that actually hinder the message of Christ.

We realized how easy it is to twist Jesus' words in ways that actually hinder the message of Christ. While we valued community, we did not seek isolation. Although the government did not always act in our personal best interests, we acknowledged that sewage systems, public schools, roads, social services, garbage collection, and public libraries were to our benefit. Paying income taxes, we felt, was part of our obligation as citizens, allowing all to enjoy the benefits of a healthy and safe society.

In Jesus' time, Israel was an occupied territory of the Roman Empire, ruled by the god-emperor Caesar. As Christians living simultaneously in God's kingdom and in a secular, human regime, all of us struggle to discern how God calls us to use our income; we all must strive to follow God's law, without breaking the laws of this world. Once again, Jesus does not give us the pat, yes/no response we may wish for. Rather, he presents another set of questions with which we must wrestle. As Jacob found in his wrestling with God (Genesis 32:22-32), such a struggle can fundamentally change us for life.

INTEGRATING

1. Over the centuries, it has proven far too easy for a charismatic individual to convince others that the end is near, that the government is evil, that isolation from the "world" is the only way to remain pure and holy. Since this is not what Jesus taught, why do so many fall prey to such messages?

2. Jesus says, "[Give] to God the things that are God's." What are the things that are God's? Is it possible to give what is God's to God?

3. When we "give to the emperor the things that are the emperor's" (that is, pay our taxes), how tempting is it to feel we have fulfilled our Christian obligation to help the poor and needy among us? How do you think God sees taxes? What is the difference between taxes, tithes, and charitable giving? How might we distinguish between these things as we share our wealth with others?

CLOSING

Stand in a circle and join hands. Have a minute or two of silence for each woman to consider how she gives to God. As you feel comfortable, share your thoughts with one another.

ELEVEN

Who Will Inherit?

READING: Luke 10:29-37

OVERVIEW

In this famous passage, Jesus answers the question of a lawyer who agrees that God wants him to love his neighbor but still wants to know "Who is my neighbor?" Jesus tells a story in which a surprising answer is revealed. It is the despised foreigner, the Samaritan—not the priest or the Levite—who has mercy on a man victimized by robbers. Both of the men see the victim, but do nothing to assist him. Now Jesus asks the lawyer which of the three was a neighbor to the victim. The lawyer answers, "The one who had mercy on him," which was the Samaritan. Jesus responds that the lawyer must behave like the Samaritan. Taken in context, this behavior, mercy, is key to the "eternal life," which the lawyer is seeking (v. 25).

VISUAL: a piece of deep-red cloth and rolls of bandages, splints, and/or other first aid items such as antibiotic ointment or iodine; with coins, cash, and a credit card scattered over it

GATHERING

When my husband and I were growing up in the United States, our families did not have health insurance. This was not a problem because, in those days, healthcare was relatively inexpensive. Today several of our five children and their families have no health insurance or have gone for significant periods without it. I now see this as a serious problem because it has the potential to ruin them financially. Medical costs are astronomical, yet the cost of health insurance premiums is out of reach for many young families. While Canada has universal healthcare for its citizens, medical costs are increasing, covered services are being slowly reduced, and waiting lists for nonemergency care are getting longer.

On both sides of the border, we citizens do not want our tax burden to rise while our coverage and our medical options decline. Yet I think of that question so popular a few years back, WWJD—What would Jesus do? If Jesus were incarnate in our society, would he be able to afford health insurance? Probably not. Would he advocate that people help pay the medical costs of strangers? Based on this story, he probably would.

DEEPENING

It is easy for us to dismiss the idea of paying for a stranger's healthcare because it is so expensive. Yet in this story, we are told that the Samaritan gave the innkeeper about two days' wages for the care of the wounded man. Would any of us be willing to pay two days' wages to meet the needs of a stranger? To some, the time that all of this care and attention would take out of an already-packed-full schedule would be an even more valuable loss than the money it would cost. But the Samaritan does more than give time and money for the immediate care of this stranger. He also tells the innkeeper to see that the victim continues to get the care he needs; any additional costs would be covered. This is like giving a credit card number to a motel clerk, with authorization to charge any costs that turn up after checkout time.

Most would not devote this kind of time and money for anyone but their own family or close friends.

Is it any wonder this story is so famous? The Samaritan is incredibly kind and generous, with both his time and his money, to someone who is a complete stranger. Most North Americans would not devote this kind of time and money for anyone but their own family or close friends.

If this is the level of generosity that we are expected to achieve, how will anyone "inherit eternal life"? Jesus seems to say that if we love God with all our mind, all our heart, and all our strength (v. 27), we will meet this requirement. Perhaps Jesus' real point is that we should examine our willingness to share both time and money with the poor and needy among us.

INTEGRATING

1. Which is easier for you—to write a check or to give of your time as a volunteer in your area? Discuss why you answer the way you do.

2. Do you think God really expects us to be as generous with others as God has been with us? What do you think the world would be like if every Christian lived this way?

CLOSING

Take a few moments to think about the many blessings God has given you, not because you are worthy, but because God loves you unconditionally. Write today's date on a piece of paper. Then, write down one gift of time and money that you would be willing to share from your abundance with a total stranger—someone you do not expect to return the favor at another time. Allow time for women to share their responses if they wish. Invite everyone to put their piece of paper in their purse or Bible. Ask them to notice how long it takes from today's date until the act is accomplished. Plan to share these experiences at a later date.

TWELVE

A Life Worth Living

READING: 1 Timothy 6:6-10, 17-19

OVERVIEW

Today's reading is a letter of instruction to Timothy, a young pastor striving to carry out the work that Paul, incarcerated in Rome, is no longer able to do. The letter encourages Timothy in teaching others in his flock, training leaders, and so forth. Here, at the end of the letter, we find warnings and directives concerning wealth. The love of money, the writer says, is the root of all evil. Accordingly, Timothy should remember that those who are not wealthy are to be content with what God has given them, while those who are rich must be humble, remembering to trust in God for everything. Both groups are to share what they have with those in need. A generous attitude enables us to live a life that is truly worth living.

VISUAL: a small quilt with several bills of money scattered over it, and a large ball of yarn

GATHERING

As a child I heard adults say many times that "money is the root of all evil." They also said it to me when I asked for money to buy special things for myself. It does not take long for young children to understand that money can be the vehicle for getting lots of stuff. Many children decide that the stuff is really the only thing worth working for in life.

I know a woman who developed this attitude as a child. As a young woman, her attitude was that she needed to pursue a husband who made a great deal of money so that she

It does not take long for young children to understand that money can be the vehicle for getting lots of stuff.

could buy whatever she wanted for her own comfort and pleasure. She has succeeded in her pursuit; her husband has achieved more wealth than she had ever dreamed of. But that is all they have to show for an entire lifetime of misery, and her marriage has been a living nightmare. Unfortunately, this is a picture of the empty life of many North Americans—in contrast to the life mentioned in today's Scripture. There are many who are wealthy in material goods, but poverty-stricken in things of the spirit. Could this emptiness be contributing to the rampant depression of both adults and children in North America?

DEEPENING

In this passage we are not chastised for being wealthy. Instead, the author tells us that the "love of money" is what causes problems. And yet, how do we discern if we love money or not? Love, like anything of importance in our lives, takes a great deal of time. We might ask ourselves how much time we devote to the accumulation and spending of money for ourselves and our families. If work is our first priority, then we may need to assess our attitude. Of course, work is necessary and should be important to us, but not only for the sake of money. Ideally, work should come out of a call to use the gifts God has given us to work for God's coming kingdom.

We might also evaluate the amount of time and energy we devote to investing money and spending money. Shopping can become a second occupation for some people, considering the amount of time it consumes. What is our attitude as we shop? Do we feel a sense of empowerment? A sense of being better than others who cannot afford to purchase the quality or quantity of goods that we can?

This passage warns us that that our wealth can be gone in an instant. Our acknowledgement that everything we have comes from God, either directly or indirectly, allows us to see wealth as a gift that we can enjoy. God also wants us to share this gift with those who were created equal in God's eyes but who have less. Our role is not to be sure others will use what we share in ways we think are appropriate, but just to share. If we do not give freely and lovingly to others, we may not be using our wealth in a way that God considers appropriate. The kind of generosity to which God calls us keeps us faithful, while letting God judge how others respond to our generosity. This is a life that is really worth living.

INTEGRATING

1. What does it mean to love money? How can you know if you love money or the material things it buys?

2. Have you ever refused to give to a person in need because you suspected they would not use what you gave in the "right" way? To what extent is this response a way of justifying our refusal to share what God has so generously given to us?

3. Tell stories of women you know who embody the contentment that comes from a transformation in their relationship with wealth.

4. Try singing "They'll Know We Are Christians by Our Love" but substituting the words "and they'll know we are Christians by how we shop." How might these words challenge your spending habits?

CLOSING

Stand in a circle. Have one person take the ball of yarn from the visual display and, holding the end of the yarn in one hand, toss the ball of yarn to someone else in the circle. As you toss the yarn to each other in this way, share how you feel connected to the person to whom you are tossing the yarn. Make sure the ball is tossed only once to each person. After each person has had the ball thrown to her, the yarn will create a web of connections visually illustrating how we are all part of one large whole community. Ask each person to remember this image, and to share generously with others, who are really a part of themselves.

THIRTEEN

Closing Worship

VISUAL FOCUS

Display the symbols from all the previous sessions on tables at the side of the room, with a circle of chairs in the middle of the room. Place a small table inside the chair circle, with a large, lit candle in a shallow pan of water on top of it. Place a small basket with a votive candle for each person near the pan. Candles may be battery operated, if preferred.

GATHERING

Leader: The closing worship invites us to consider anew the blessing of money God has given us, and encourage us to follow God's urging to fulfill the responsibilities this blessing requires. Take a few moments to walk around the room and look at the symbols used in these sessions. Consider one that has been especially meaningful to you.

Praising

Luke 4:18-21

Giving thanks

Each person may light a tealight candle and place it in the pan of water to float around the large candle. As she lights it, she may share with the group something she is thankful for.

Psalm 92:1-2

Leader: It is good to give thanks to the LORD,

People: to sing praises to your name, O Most High;

Leader: to declare your steadfast love in the morning

People: and your faithfulness by night.

All: Amen.

CONFESSING

Psalm 51:1, 10, 12

Leader: Have mercy on me, O God, according to your steadfast love;

People: according to your abundant mercy blot out my transgressions.

(silence)

Leader: Create in me a clean heart, O God, and put a new and right spirit within me.

People: Restore to me the joy of your salvation and sustain in me a willing spirit.

All: Amen.

LISTENING

Scripture readings

Reader 1: Mark 6:34-44

Reader 2: 2 Kings 4:42-44

Reader 3: Malachi 3:7b-10, 12

(Reflect silently on the readings.)

RESPONDING

Share with each other, as it is comfortable, about the symbol from the sessions that is most meaningful. Explain why.

Response prayer

Reader 1: We give you thanks, O God, for your wonderful generosity.

Reader 2: You have provided richly for our enjoyment.

Reader 3: May we, in turn, be rich in good works, generous, and ready to share.

All: Hear our prayer, O God.

(Pause for silent prayer.)

Reader 1: We give you thanks, O God, for your many provisions.

Reader 2: We brought nothing into the world and we will take nothing out of it.

Reader 3: Help us to be content with what we have.

All: Hear our prayer, O God.

(Pause for silent prayer.)

Reader 1: We give you thanks, O God, for our neighbors near and far.

Reader 2: We remember the difficulties many encounter throughout life.

Reader 3: Help us to show mercy to all.

All: Hear our prayer, O God.

(Pause for silent prayer.)

Reader 1: May we take hold of the life that is really life.

Reader 2: May we always seek the kingdom of God.

Reader 3: Amen.

SENDING

Benediction

2 Thessalonians 3:16, 17b

Leader: Now may the Lord of peace himself give you peace at all times in all ways. The Lord be with all of you. The grace of our Lord Jesus Christ be with all of you.

People: And also with you.

All: Amen.

About the Writer

PATRICIA BURDETTE is married to Rob Burdette, and they are parents of five children and several grandchildren. She considers the responsibilities of motherhood to be the most significant as well as the most joyful endeavor of her life. She and her husband, three children, and their families live in various dwellings on their rural Ohio organic "farmette."

Patty was a financial development and public relations professional prior to beginning volunteer service assignments with Mennonite Central Committee (MCC). For six years she and her family served in Saskatchewan with projects related to aboriginal concerns. They served another six years in North Dakota among the Lakota on the Pine Ridge Reservation.

After serving with MCC, Patty completed a doctoral degree, and taught English literature, rhetoric, composition, and American Indian studies courses for over twenty years. She is now retired.

More titles in the

ABUNDANT

Faith

WOMEN'S BIBLE
STUDY SERIES

Courageous Women
Strong. Courageous. Persistent. Uncover stories of biblical women who acted with unflinching courage—women who sought justice, spoke truth, and witnessed to God's love. The women profiled in this Bible study serve as models to encourage and challenge us today.

Generous Gifts
Scripture reveals a God who has lavished many gifts upon us in creation, healing, and relationships. In gratitude, we join God in offering healing and hope to the world. This Bible study helps us appreciate the full range of God's goodness to us, and to discern creative ways to share our gifts wherever God has placed us.

Wonderfully Made
To offer good and healthy care to others, we need to nurture and replenish ourselves. Using wisdom learned from her journey with infertility, the writer connects with readers and their own life experiences by using sound scriptural and psychological principles helpful in self-care. This Bible study validates the importance of personal wholeness.

CPSIA information can be obtained at www.ICGtesting.com
Printed in the USA
BVOW02s2108200116

433684BV00001B/11/P

9 781513 800257